THE LABONTE BROTHERS

Jeff Burton

Dale Earnhardt Jr.

Famous Finishes

Famous Tracks

Kenny Irwin Jr.

Jimmie Johnson

The Labonte Brothers

Lowriders

Monster Trucks & Tractors

Motorcycles

Off-Road Racing

Rockcrawling

Tony Stewart

The Unsers

Rusty Wallace

THE LABONTE
BROTHERS

Janet Hubbard-Brown

CHELSEA HOUSE PUBLISHERS

Cover Photo: NASCAR legends and brothers Bobby Labonte (left) and Terry Labonte savor their unique double victory in the NAPA 500 on November 10, 1996 at the Atlanta Motor Speedway in Hampton, Georgia. Bobby won the race, and Terry's fifth place finish earned him the Winston Cup Championship.

CHELSEA HOUSE PUBLISHERS

VP, NEW PRODUCT DEVELOPMENT   Sally Cheney
DIRECTOR OF PRODUCTION   Kim Shinners
CREATIVE MANAGER   Takeshi Takahashi
MANUFACTURING MANAGER   Diann Grasse

STAFF FOR THE LABONTE BROTHERS

EDITORIAL ASSISTANT Sarah Sharpless
PRODUCTION EDITOR Bonnie Cohen
PHOTO EDITOR Pat Holl
SERIES DESIGN AND LAYOUT Hierophant Publishing Services/EON PreMedia

http://www.chelseahouse.com

First Printing

1   3   5   7   9   8   6   4   2

Library of Congress Cataloging-in-Publication Data

Hubbard-Brown, Janet
    The Labonte brothers / Janet Hubbard-Brown.
        p. cm.—(Race car legends. Collector's edition)
    Includes bibliographical references and index.
    ISBN 0-7910-8767-0
    1. Labonte, Terry, 1956—Juvenile literature. 2. Labonte, Bobby, 1964—Juvenile literature. 3. Stock car drivers—United States—Biography—Juvenile literature. I. Title. II. Series.
GV1032.A1H817 2005
796.72'09'2—dc22

                                                                2005014465

TABLE OF CONTENTS

① DOUBLE CHAMPIONS

No one who saw it will ever forget the Winston Cup Series (now known as the Nextel Cup Series) NAPA 500 race that took place in Hampton, Georgia, on November 11, 1996.

It was the last Cup race of the season and an important one for Terry Labonte, because if he finished eighth or better, he would win the 1996 NASCAR (National Association for Stock Car Auto Racing) Cup Championship, worth over one million dollars. But what felt more important than the money was that Terry was winning again. He had won the Cup Championship in 1984 and now was on the verge of winning again. During those 12 years of not achieving his goal, he had learned how to be consistent, patient, and calm. During that time he was nicknamed "The Iceman." On November 16, he would be turning 40.

His brother Bobby, eight years younger, was in the pole position, which is the first car on the left inside the two columns. That position goes to the driver who wins the qualifying races preceding the Sunday race. Bobby could look in his rearview mirror and see his brother, who was starting in third position.

Bobby had been racing in the Cup Series for only four years. Until 1990, he had spent most of his time racing in the NASCAR Busch Grand National Series, which is one level below the Cup Series. It is considered a good training ground for big-time racers.

By the time he entered the race at Atlanta Motor Speedway, Terry had 4,657 points under his belt. Drivers received points throughout the year for finishing first, second, and so on. Bonus points were awarded for leading a lap in a race, and for leading the most number of laps in a race. Points were even earned for finishing a race. With this point system, NASCAR rewarded those who did well consistently, coming in second or third, rather than those who won big and lost big. The team that got crowned was the one that had the best overall performance. The two drivers Terry had to beat to win the Cup were the young rookie Jeff Gordon, who was only 47 points behind him, and Dale Jarrett.

Sunday, the day of the race, began early. The brothers waited while their cars were inspected. NASCAR officials have ruined race days for many drivers because of mistakes that have to do with the car. They want to make sure there is no cheating.

Three cars were being raced that day: the Ford Thunderbird, which was replaced by the Taurus in 1998; the Chevy Monte Carlo, which Terry Labonte was driving; and the Pontiac Grand Prix, which was Bobby's car.

The first order of business was to meet with the cars' owners and crew chiefs. Rick Hendrick owned Terry's car and Joe Gibbs owned Bobby's car. The crew chief today is considered perhaps the most important person on the team next to the driver. He has to be a mechanic, a coach, and a manager. But most important, there has to be a good chemistry between the driver and his crew chief.

Bobby and Terry next met with their fans and signed autographs. NASCAR drivers are known to relate well to

Bobby Labonte, driving the green Interstate Batteries car, leads his brother, Terry Labonte, through Turn 4 during the NAPA 500 NASCAR event at Atlanta Motor Speedway in Hampton, Georgia. Bobby went on to win the race, and Terry finished fifth to become the 1996 Cup champion.

their fans. Two hours before the race, they gathered with their crew chiefs and NASCAR officials. Their families joined them for a brief prayer service.

Then all of the drivers walked out to face a stadium filled with 140,000 cheering fans. Terry wore a bright red and yellow firesuit that had green stripes. His sponsor was Kellogg's and that company's logo was written on the sleeves of his suit and across the hood of his car. He was driving car No. 5, a Chevrolet Monte Carlo. Bobby wore black and green to match his lime-green Pontiac, car No. 18, decorated with the words "Interstate Batteries." They and the 41 other drivers entered their race cars through the driver's side window, reaching back to close the netting that fits over the window. If there is an accident, the driver removes the netting, which tells everyone that he is okay.

Bobby Labonte had said to his family only the night before how neat it would be if Terry could clinch the title and he himself could win the race. He knew that the chance of that happening was very slim. Terry was driving under a handicap that day in Hampton, Georgia because he had broken a bone in his left hand racing in Phoenix a few weeks before. The throttle had hung open and he had hit the wall, breaking his hand. For the next two races, he had to drive with a splint on his hand, leaving only three fingers free to grip the wheel.

The command was issued: "Drivers, start your engines!" Seconds before, the drivers had tripped several toggle switches to place themselves in the ready position. Next, they hit the switch that turns the engine over. The second the command came over the loudspeaker, they pressed the start switch. In that instant, the driver has close to 700-plus horsepower at his command and his car can reach 65 miles per hour in low gear. It doesn't take long to reach 200 miles per hour.

Terry and Bobby Labonte had 328 laps to travel before a winner would be declared. Bobby's closest pursuer was Jeff Gordon. On Lap 108, Gordon took the lead, but he couldn't keep it. On Lap 281, Bobby gained the third spot and passed Jeff Gordon. He passed Ricky Rudd on Lap 286, and on Lap 287 he passed Bobby Hamilton. He was ahead for the next 42 circuits. When the checkered flag went down (meaning the race was over), Bobby had beaten Dale Jarrett by only 0.41 second. His brother's car loomed large in the rearview mirror. It felt like a miracle.

Terry Labonte (center left) and team owner Rick Hendrick (center right) celebrate their win of the 1996 Cup points trophy. Terry's record of consistently finishing well throughout the season paid off handsomely.

Terry had run steadily. At one point toward the end of the race, he was advised by his crew that he could not make the distance with the fuel he had remaining. During the race, many caution flags had been thrown and drivers had to slow down because of an accident, rain, or debris on the track. A caution gives those in the rear a chance to catch up because no one can pass until the yellow flag is replaced by the green, signaling that the race has started again. Terry decided to go for it because a pit stop would put him out of the running.

When Terry came off Turn 4 he knew the championship that he had been dreaming of for 12 years was his once

DID YOU KNOW?

Cheating Happens

Did you know that cheating used to be common among race car drivers? Within the closely knit community of NASCAR stock car racers, cheating is an acknowledged part of the sport, though one that is rarely discussed in the polite company of outsiders, especially for the record.*

In order to have the fastest car, drivers would add or delete parts or make other changes that weren't legal. Today, NASCAR inspectors not only check the cars before the race but can do random checks throughout the race. They check everything from tires to rear spoilers. No one wants to pay a fine of up to $50,000 for being caught with an illegal engine, or with a part not approved by NASCAR.

The first time cheating was made public was when car owner and former racer Junior Johnson was caught at Daytona in 1995. He brought in an illegal manifold that allowed in more air, which increased the car's horse-power.**

Mark Martin lost the 1990 Cup championship over an intake manifold spacer that had been bolted rather than welded in place. His car owner, Jack Roush, still gets emotional when he talks about the injustice of it.

*Tom Jenson, *Cheating: An Inside Look at the Bad Things Good NASCAR Nextel Cup Racers Do in Pursuit of Speed.* Phoenix, AZ: David Bull Publishing, 2004, p. 10.

**Shaun Assael, *Wide Open: Days and Nights on the NASCAR Tour.* New York, NY: Ballantine Books, 1998, p. 63.

again. The roar of the crowd was deafening. The two brothers took a spontaneous, slow victory lap, side by side. Terry's voice cracked with emotion when asked how it felt to win: "It just really, really makes you feel good. My wife, my kids, everybody . . . . It just about got me. That's the first time I've gotten emotional. I was a little surprised at myself. That was really special, to see those people and the happiness I saw on their faces."[1]

Bobby made $274,900 for winning the NAPA 500. Terry was handed a check for $1.5 million for winning the championship. The Labonte boys had come a long way from their Corpus Christi, Texas, roots, when keeping Terry racing was a financial challenge for the family.

"What a cool deal," Bobby said, recalling that race. "There in Victory Lane were Rick Hendrick, Joe Gibbs, Terry and I and Mom and Dad . . . . it was a monumental day. Our parents won twice that day—their kids won both deals. You can't go to Victory Lane with both your kids on that day. It was just unbelievable."[2]

② ON THE ROAD

Terry and Bobby Labonte's mother, Martha, who thinks of herself as shy and quiet, likes to say that her oldest son is like her, and her youngest is more like his father Bob, who is outgoing and entertaining.

Bob Labonte developed a passionate interest in cars when he was growing up in Maine. He raced 1935 Fords and worked on race cars in his spare time. After joining the Navy, he was assigned to the Corpus Christi Naval Station. It was there that he met Martha, who grew up in south Texas. Bob continued to work for the government, but spent an equal amount of time in the garage next to his house working on cars.

Terry was born in 1956. By the time he entered first grade, his father's love of racing and cars had been instilled in him. "I put him in a go-kart almost before he could write his name," Terry's father said.[3]

Martha Labonte recalls the first time Terry's father put him in a quarter midget, a child-size open car. He encouraged him to race around a track. Terry's cautious nature was already evident—he insisted on doing a practice run first. His mother worried that Bob was pushing him, but they soon discovered that Terry didn't need any pushing. He was a natural.

13

He was also a quiet, observant child who was doted on by his parents. Terry's close friend, Slick Yoemans, who is five years older, laughs when he recalls that Terry had a hard time staying at school as a first-grader. "By the time his mama got home, Terry was already there," Yeomans said.[4]

When he was 7, Bob and Martha gave their first-born a quarter midget of his own. A year later, Bobby was born. The Labontes traveled all over the country so Terry could race the quarter midgets. They went to San Antonio, Texas; Portland, Maine; and Tucson, Arizona. Racing was now a family passion. Bobby, at age 2, had already adapted to the lifestyle of a race car driver. Whether in a car or out, drivers are constantly in motion.

Slick Yoemans raced with Terry in Corpus Christi at a track across from the salvage yard where he worked. During the middle of one race, a fire broke out at the salvage yard. Everybody stopped and ran to put out the fire, then returned to finish the race. Terry was called "Fireball" after that.[5]

Bob remembers when Terry wanted to play football. "He also said he wanted to be in real estate sales because those people all wear big rings and drive big cars," he laughed.[6]

When he was in high school, Terry's parents drove him to Houston on weekends to race, then drove the four hours back home. He raced quarter midgets until he was 15, when he grew too big for them. Then he switched to late model cars, which were usually found in salvage yards and "souped up" for racing.

One weekend, the Labontes could not afford to buy the tires Terry needed for a race in Houston. They decided not to go, even though Terry had won the point standings. The owner of the track called and asked if he could get Terry a sponsor. A

Terry Labonte is shown inside his NASCAR Nextel Cup Series car surrounded by safety devices such as the seat belts/ straps, strap netting over the entryway, and side impact pads, which are part of the seat.

wealthy Louisiana oilman named Billy Hagen entered Terry's life in a stroke of luck that changed everything. He had seen Terry race and liked what he saw. Terry had won nine out of eleven races. Hagen guaranteed Terry $1,000 a night.

Terry met his bride-to-be, Kim, in 1973, when they both worked at a used car lot in Corpus Christi. He was 16 and she was 17. She was quiet and serious like Terry. One of her favorite memories is of their first date, when he took her out to a great restaurant and gave her a bracelet. She still has it today.

Terry went to North Carolina under Hagen's umbrella to work in a pit crew. His mother remembers that they all cried

NASCAR Is a Family Business

From its earliest beginnings in 1947, NASCAR has prided itself on being a family business that sells strong family values. The organization has remained under the ownership of one family, the France family, which is remarkable in today's corporate world.

Racing is in the genes. The proof of that is the number of siblings and fathers and sons who race side by side. The Labonte brothers are the only set of brothers who have both won the Cup championship. Other sets of racing brothers are Darrell and Michael Waltrip; Bobby and Donnie Allison; Jeff and Ward Burton; Geoff, Brett, and Todd Bodine; David and Jeff Green; Rusty, Kenny, and Mike Wallace; and the current most famous set of brothers, Kyle and Kurt Busch.

The Petty family and the Earnhardt families have operated as dynasties. Four generations of Pettys have raced. Dale Jarrett is the son of two-time champion Ned Jarrett. Dale's brother is Glenn Jarrett and he is the father of Jason Jarrett, another young driver who is making waves. Eight-time winner Sterling Marlin is the son of driver Coo Coo Marlin.

Aside from the Labontes, other drivers with kids coming up are Bobby Hamilton, Jimmy Spencer, Mike Skinner, and Geoff Bodine. What they have all learned is that a brother's or father's names might get them in the door, but it won't keep them there. It is up to them to prove themselves.

when he left—"all except Bobby," she corrected herself—"because he could now move into Terry's room and have a telephone."[7]

For Terry, being part of a pit crew was an opportunity for him to learn the ropes of car racing from the bottom up. Pit crew members have to change tires, fill gas tanks, and clean windshields in record time. The faster they complete their tasks, the better their drivers do in the overall standings. It was dangerous work. During one race, three members of the Hagen pit crew, including Terry, ended up with broken legs when a racer came in too fast.

Terry was an enthusiastic, fast learner in his hands-on job. Some say today that Terry could build a race car from scratch because he is so knowledgeable about every part of the car. The same is true for Bobby.

Living in North Carolina was the first time Terry had been away from home for any length of time. He became homesick. His folks in Corpus Christi, along with Kim, also missed him. They decided to travel to North Carolina to visit him in 1978. It was a decision that would change all their lives.

③

TERRY'S FIRST CHAMPIONSHIP

Terry's parents, Bob and Martha, went to their first big Daytona race—the Super Bowl of races—in 1978. They also visited their son in North Carolina. For the Labontes, racing had always been a family commitment, and during that visit Bob and Martha decided to move to North Carolina to be near their oldest son. Bobby would be entering ninth grade.

Kim and Terry were married on May 25, 1978. Terry made his racing debut that same year at the Southern 500 in Darlington, South Carolina. Darlington Raceway is considered one of the most difficult racetracks in the country.

There are different styles of tracks. The Atlanta Motor Speedway is an intermediate track that runs from 1 to 2 miles in length. Other types of tracks include superspeedways (Daytona and Talladega) that run 2 miles or longer, short tracks that run one-half to three-quarters of a mile in length, and road tracks (Sears Point in California and Watkins Glen in New York) that contain hairpin curves and straightaways. Later, when Bobby decided he wanted to race, Terry would coach him to memorize the tracks, for each requires specific driving tactics.

Terry came in fourth at Darlington. In that year, he was in five races and won $20,545. In 1979 he was runner-up to Dale Earnhardt Sr. for the Rookie of the Year award. Victory did not come, however, until 1980, when he won at Darlington in the Southern 500. He won a pole in 1981 at the Atlanta Coca-Cola 500. Between 1979 and 1984, Terry competed in 184 races, winning only four of them. But he had acquired an excellent record for finishing either in the "top ten" or the "top five," which marked the beginning of a continuing reputation for consistency. The points were mounting, and there was talk that Terry might be in the running for a championship in the near future. The money also was beginning to accumulate. In 1982, for example, Terry ran 30 races and won $363,970.

Terry and Kim's son, Justin, was born in 1981, and in 1982, a daughter, Kristen ("Kristy"), arrived. It was at this stage in his life that Terry experienced his first and only serious accident as a race car driver. It happened in 1982 in the final Cup race in Riverside, California. A tire went flat, and when Terry tried to turn his car to the right, it went straight into the wall. According to people who were there, his car never even touched the racetrack.

It took Terry a month to recover from the injuries he suffered in that accident: a broken leg, a broken foot, some broken ribs, a broken nose, and severe cuts on his face. It was the only time he questioned his choice of career. As he began to heal, however, he knew that racing would always be his life. He was relieved that it had been the last race of the season, which would give him time to mend without missing any races.

Martha and Kim were visiting family and friends in Texas when the accident happened. It was a 24-hour drive back to North Carolina. Martha recalled that it was the longest drive of her life.[8]

Terry Labonte holds his son Justin, 4 years old, and the Busch Clash Trophy after winning the race in Daytona Beach, Florida. On the right are Labonte's wife, Kim, and their 20-month-old daughter, Kristen.

Terry was ready when the new season started. Every waking moment was focused on his career. In 1983, he was fifth in the point standings. He had two wins in 1984—one at the Bristol International Raceway (now known as the Bristol Motor Speedway) and the other at the Riverside International Raceway. He was in the top five 17 times and was in the top ten 24 times. On November 18, 1984, the Labonte family's dream came true: Terry won the Cup championship in Hagen's late model 1957 Chevy. He won $713,010 that year.

Terry's future could not have seemed brighter that day. He was the declared champion. His younger brother Bobby

DID YOU KNOW?

Adrenaline: Speed Is an Addiction

Sixty-one year old drag racer Eddie Hill said, "It [winning at speed] feels so good it's unbelievable. It's extremely habit-forming, and incurable. You can cure people of all kinds of addictions, but you can't cure anybody of this."* The driver is referring to the sensation of flying around a track at 180 to 200 miles an hour.

This might have something to do with why the older drivers are having a hard time giving it up. Lee Montgomery wrote, "Making it tougher is that drivers are a lot like addicts. They can't get race cars out of their system, no matter how hard they try."** Mark Martin declared he would "walk 100 miles barefoot through snow to achieve it."***

According to author G. Wayne Miller, adrenaline hooks many young drivers, but it doesn't help when it comes to winning races. More experienced drivers strive to enter a state that isn't about adrenaline taking over. Their pulse, respiration, and perspiration increase when rounding turns. They are responding to the G-forces, the heat of the cockpit, and the effort of steering. Their concentration becomes much greater, their reflexes faster, their eyesight keener, and their thinking clearer. Basically, it is what is often referred to as a "runner's high."

*G. Wayne Miller, *Men and Speed: A Wild Ride through NASCAR's Breakout Season*. New York, NY: Public Affairs, 2002, p. 141.

**Lee Montgomery, "Changing of the Guard: *As Older Drivers Depart, Young Stars Are Filling the Void*," *The News & Observer*, February 12, 2004, p. 1 C.

***Miller, p. 31.

Terry Labonte poses with his first victory trophy after winning the Southern 500 at Darlington Raceway, South Carolina, September 1, 1980.

and his father were working at Hagen's shop, and he was surrounded by family. The championship would be a springboard for the many wins that lay ahead. The Labontes were not wrong in that prediction, but no one thought it would take as long as it did. And they didn't know then that Bobby would follow in his brother's footsteps.

4

HE'S NEVER MET A STRANGER

"**H**e's never met a stranger," Martha Labonte said when asked about Bobby.[9]

A teacher from Trinity High School in Trinity, North Carolina, Beverly Crotts, remembers Bobby well. She was pleased to have the opportunity to say how friendly and easy-going he was: "He used to come up to my desk and talk and talk," she says.[10] Terry Labonte's son, Justin, now 24, attended the same high school, and Crotts thinks he is just like his Uncle Bobby.

Bobby followed in his brother's footsteps in Corpus Christi, racing quarter midgets and go-karts. The Labontes lived across from the elementary school there. Martha and Bob Labonte would set out jugs and encourage Bobby to practice going around them when he was only 4 years old. One day, little Bobby was out in his go-kart practicing, when his mother noticed that his head was dropping lower and lower. "I think he's going to sleep out there," she said.[11] She took the tired little boy inside.

In 1970, Bobby was taken to a race in Maine. After racing around and around the track, he stopped, got out of his

Bobby Labonte, August 1995, waits for practice to start at the Michigan International Speedway in Brooklyn, Michigan. Terry Labonte's easy-going brother got his start working as a mechanic for Billy Hagen's Race team.

car, and ran to his parents. "Did I win?" the innocent child asked. He had in fact won his first national quarter midget race.

Bobby was the tagalong brother. From his earliest years, the family did much the same as they do today: travel from race to race. Racing was in Bobby's blood. When Terry got a stock car to race, his parents put all their effort into his career efforts. Bobby didn't race much for a while, even though he

Car Racers Are Athletes

No question can annoy a car racer more than being asked if he considers himself an athlete. The answer, in case you didn't know, is yes.

A study was done in 2002 on Indy-style Championship Auto Racing Teams (CART) that offers final proof. Drivers tested had physical fitness levels equal to those found previously in professional football, baseball, and basketball. The drivers burned the same energy as a runner.

"The days are gone when you can be competitive and not be in peak physical condition," Dr. Stephen E. Olvey said. He is the researcher and director of Medical Affairs for CART. The thought is that NASCAR racers would be in even better shape, because they race longer hours.

Bobby and Terry Labonte, along with the other drivers, can take advantage of a mobile workout center that travels with the Nextel Cup Series. Bobby Labonte, when home, bikes 40 miles a day. Ellott Sadler said that during a race he loses 8 to 12 pounds in fluids. It gets up to 150 degrees inside the car. He also will sit in a steam room for an hour at a time to get his lungs used to breathing hot air.*

Dodge driver Kasey Kahne said that if an average guy got into a NASCAR race car, either he wouldn't be able to drive it, or by the end of a race he would have passed out from exhaustion and heat.

* "NASCAR: Drivers take stock of their fitness," *Knight Ridder Tribune*, February 9, 2005, *www.freep.com/sports/othersports/autos9e_20050209.htm.*

Terry Labonte (left) and race car owner Billy Hagen hold the Winston Cup trophy that Terry won after placing third in the 1984 Western 500 at Riverside International Raceway near Riverside, California.

did race go-karts at age 14. That continued for two years, then he switched to late model stock cars. Within a five- or six-year period, he competed in 12 races. His mother remembers Bobby practically living at the race shop during his high school years. He swept the floors, cleaned parts, and was put in charge of ordering parts. He also worked as a fabricator.

Bobby graduated from high school in 1982, and began working full-time at Hagen Racing. He was 18 and didn't have the money to race much, so he worked as a mechanic. He worked side by side with his dad Bob. Terry continued moving up in the racing world, but Bobby didn't see how he could follow in his brother's footsteps. Racing, even then, required sponsors and a lot of money. The Labonte family felt a strong loyalty to Billy Hagen, who had given them their first big break.

Bobby was 20 when Terry won the Cup championship, fulfilling his family's hopes. The Labontes had no reason to think they wouldn't be connected to Hagen for many years to come. But surprises were in store.

5

THE BROTHERS COMPETE

After winning the 1984 Cup Championship, Terry won only one race in 1985, the Busch Clash. The Busch Series is one step below the Cup in terms of cash prizes and status. The cars themselves are slightly smaller. When his contract with Billy Hagen ran out in 1986, Terry switched over to a team that was being formed by Junior Johnson. Johnson was one of the early stars of stock car racing. Terry stayed with him for three years.

Hagen fired Bob and Bobby Labonte when Terry left. Today Bobby thinks the day Hagen fired him actually turned out to be one of his luckiest days. It was then that he knew he wanted to race.

Bobby began to come into his own in the mid-1980s, just as his brother was hitting a mid-career slump. They raced late model stock cars in 1986, and in 1987 he won the Late Model Championship at Caraway Speedway in Asheboro, North Carolina. He was 23 years old. He had 12 wins that year, seven poles, and finished in the top five 20 times in 23 races.

In 1988, Terry won the Winston Select. He had two wins in 1989: the Talladega 500 and the other at Pocono Raceway.

Bobby Labonte is shown here in 1990, the year he began racing full-time in the Busch Grand National circuit. Bobby was named Most Popular Driver that same year. By the early 1990s, he and brother Terry were competing against each other.

He also won the International Race of Champions championship. He decided to spend a year with car owner Richard Jackson, then he went back to Hagen in 1990. Terry remained there until 1993. There were no wins in those years.

Bobby Labonte poses with his wife, Donna, and their two children after winning the Cup trophy in 2000.

Bobby, in the meantime, began racing in the Late Model Sportsman Series in 1988. He moved to the Busch Series in 1990. In that same year he was named Most Popular Driver. He won the NASCAR Busch Series Grand National Division championship in 1991, but was edged out the following year.

In March of 1991, he married Donna Slate. They had met eight years earlier, soon after the Labontes had moved to Trinity. Terry and Bobby started competing with each other that year. Bobby's first Cup race was the Peak 500 race in Dover, Delaware. A man named Bill Davis was the car owner.

Now the brothers were racing against each other. Martha Labonte claims that her sons are very close, but also very competitive. They'd have to be to stay in the Cup series year after year. Any race-car driver will say that it is the winning that drives him, not the money and fame. Drivers love to compete. Terry says his favorite driver to race against is his brother. Other sets of brothers have publicly clashed, but the Labonte brothers are known for their loyalty to each other. Bobby has always called his brother Terry his hero.

The brothers do not look alike. Terry is 5 feet, 10 inches, has reddish hair, and sports a neatly trimmed mustache. Nicknamed "The Iceman" because he rarely shows emotion, he is a man of few words. Bobby, 2 inches shorter than his brother, has a childlike quality about him. He has dark brown hair, blue eyes, and an expressive smile. He is known for his dry sense of humor.

Writer Ben White described Bobby in 1995:

As with his older brother, Bobby is simple but also complex. He is shy but aggressive. He is opinionated but never overbearing. He is goal-oriented but genuine . . . . confidence radiates from him like a neon sign shining brightly on a street corner at a late-night hour.[12]

When Bobby was asked in an interview how he developed his clean driving style, he answered that "experience was a big part of it. And having 'The Iceman' as your brother and having that in your genes probably helps. I'm not a total opposite of him [Terry]. I'm a little opposite, but not in a lot of ways, or if it is, it's not necessarily on the racetrack as much as it is in my personal life. But our thought processes are similar."[13]

As Bobby moved forward in leaps and bounds, Terry tried to find his way back to a successful career. He and his wife Kim started his NASCAR Busch Series team in 1991,

Bobby Labonte (right) talks with team owner Joe Gibbs. Gibbs is famous for coaching the Washington Redskins before he became interested in racing. He was inducted into the NFL Hall of Fame in 1996.

where he ran a few events with Sunoco, an earlier sponsor. His father Bob became crew chief.

Terry continued to enter every race, determined to do his best. This attitude had been instilled in the two brothers from an early age. It paid off years later when Terry beat Richard Petty's record of entering the most consecutive races.

It was when Bobby joined Joe Gibbs Racing in 1994 that his career really kicked into gear. Bobby has said many times that his two heroes are his father and his brother. Joe Gibbs, owner of Bobby's team, is also a hero to Bobby. Before he became interested in racing, Gibbs was famous as the coach of the Washington Redskins for 11 years. He won three Super

DID YOU KNOW?

Kids Are Racing?

The drivers are getting younger at NASCAR races. Fifteen-year-old Chase Austin signed a development deal with Hendrick Motorsports in 2004. Mark Martin's 13-year-old son, Matt, is already on contract with Ford. Matt has been racing in Florida in the FastKids Series at Orlando Speedworld. Kids racing is a new trend. As drivers at NASCAR begin serious racing at 18, young kids begin dreaming of becoming NASCAR stars.

Bobby Labonte's children are both currently racing go-karts. The most famous youngsters in 2005 are the Busch brothers. Kyle Busch, the younger brother of Nextel Cup champion Kurt Busch, was under contract to Roush Racing when he was 16. Drivers have to be 18 to race.

In 2004, only one of the top 10 racers in points standings was over 35. That was Mark Martin. At the Busch Series opener at Daytona, 10 drivers were under 24 years old, including Justin Labonte.

Terry Labonte has already declared himself committed to his son Justin, now 24. Justin has been racing for years. In April, 2004, he made his first start at the O'Reilly 300 at Texas Motor Speedway. NASCAR writer Marty Smith, in a conversation, made it clear that Justin has not had everything handed to him on a silver platter the way some young drivers had. Justin had his first win at Chicagoland Speedway in July of 2004.

Bowls in 1983, 1988, and 1992, and was inducted into the NFL Hall of Fame in 1996.

In 1993 car owner Bill Davis was moving up to the Cup series with his driver Jeff Gordon. When Gordon changed his mind and decided to go with Rick Hendrick, Bobby was asked to drive the No. 22 car that had been Jeff's. Bobby ended the season as runner-up for Rookie of the Year. The top honor went to Jeff Gordon.

Donna Labonte gave birth to Tyler Labonte that same year. In 1994, Bobby added a second Busch Series title to his name, as owner of a Chevrolet driven by champion David Green. Bob Labonte helped with that. In fact, Bobby and Terry shared the same shop. Bobby holds the record of being the only driver to win the Busch Series title as a driver and then win it again as a car owner while driving for someone else.

The shop today belongs to Terry Labonte, but it is his son Justin's 2004 Busch Series car that fills the front lobby. Justin competed in 17 Busch races last year. He earned his first NASCAR victory at Chicagoland. The car in the lobby is the one he drove to victory in July of 2004. Because of that win, the Labontes were able to merge Labonte Motorsports with Haas CNC Racing, a top-ten, Hendrick Motorsports-affiliated team.[14]

Terry's luck took a dramatic change for the better when Rick Hendrick asked him to join his team in 1994. Terry's teammates were Jeff Gordon and Ricky Craven. Terry finished seventh in the final point standings that year. He now had 14 top finishes under his belt.

Bobby's first Cup victory came in the spring of 1995 when he won the Coca-Cola 600 in Charlotte, North Carolina. It was his first season with Joe Gibbs Racing. The following year he

Justin Labonte, son of Terry Labonte, is shown after winning the 2004 NASCAR Tropicana Twister 300 at Chicagoland Speedway in Joliet, Illinois.

won two big races in Michigan and one in North Carolina. He finished the season 10th in the points standing.

In 1995 Terry had three wins again, at Richmond International Raceway, Pocono Raceway, and Bristol Motor Speedway. He finished sixth in the final point standings and earned $1,125,921. He was back on top. All the hard work climbing there—the jobs, the hundreds of races, the disappointments, the concern over money—had been worth it.

Little did the Labonte brothers dream, even then, that in the near future the competition for young drivers to make an impression on the television audience would be so great that some would be signed while they were still children. In another decade Terry's and Bobby's hard-work ethic and modesty would seem old-fashioned in the ever-changing world of NASCAR.

But Bobby wasn't done winning yet, and neither was Terry.

6

BROTHERS MAKE HISTORY

Terry's winning the Cup Championship in 1984 and 1996 had brought him more success than he had dreamed of, but it was a race in 1997 that had a lasting emotional impact on those who witnessed it. It was the Daytona 500, the race that starts the season each year. It is the most publicized of all stock car races.

The race took place on February 22. Terry Labonte, Jeff Gordon, and Ricky Craven were teammates under Rick Hendrick of Hendrick Motorsports. Rick had been drawn to racing most of his adult life. As he progressed in his career, he provided emotional and financial support to many. He had made his fortune in Honda car dealerships.

Hendrick had been diagnosed with a rare form of leukemia months earlier. It had been devastating news for his family and friends.

On the day of the Daytona 500, Rick's three drivers entered the race determined to win for him. Jeff Gordon had not managed to win the Daytona 500 in the past four years. He had been on such a winning streak since he entered the racing world, however, that the young driver was considered a major star. He, Terry, and Craven would be racing against Dale

Earnhardt Sr., who was more determined than ever to break his bad-luck streak of never winning the Daytona 500. On top of that, none of the three Hendrick drivers had won in the qualifying races the day before.

That Daytona 500 was a race of passion, luck (both good and bad), and incredible driving skills. On Lap 110, Gordon had tire trouble. He had to pit and lost nearly a full lap, dropping from 3rd place to 31st. He was 25 years old, racing against men who were much older. He was in despair by the time he got back on the track.

Mark Martin tried to pass Gordon but could not. A caution flag came up on Lap 122 and Gordon caught up. With only 11 laps to go, Bill Elliott was in the lead, with Dale Earnhardt Sr. right behind. Then Earnhardt saw Gordon approaching in his rearview mirror. They were at Turn 2, and Gordon rushed up beside Earnhardt. Earnhardt would not give in. Then it happened. Earnhardt's Chevy hit the wall at 190 miles per hour, bounced off, and hit Gordon's Chevy. Dale Jarrett and Ernie Irvan also got caught up in the accident. Terry Labonte ran into the back of Irvan. The caution flag waved again.

Terry had started 18th and stayed in 10th place until midway through the race. Then everything started to change. Terry and Ricky Craven came up behind Jeff Gordon, but Bill Elliott was still in the lead.

Jeff tuned into Labonte's two-way radio channel and suggested that they get the three Hendrick cars past Elliott. Terry thought it was a good idea. Jeff then tuned to Ricky's channel and told him that Terry was going with him. Ricky said he was going with him, too.

Elliott later said, "With three Hendrick cars behind you, you ain't got a chance. I was dead meat, and I knew it. It was just a matter of where and when."[15]

Dale Earnhardt Sr. hits the wall and flips during the 1997 Daytona 500. Ernie Irvan (No. 28) and Dale Jarrett (No. 88) are also pictured. Terry Labonte's car (not clearly visible in this photo) is about to strike Irvan's car.

At Lap 194, when they came to Turn 1, the three Monte Carlos started to make their moves. Gordon went left, and Labonte and Craven went high up on the banking on the right and sailed past. Their strategy worked.

The Hendrick team crosses the finish line 1-2-3 at the Daytona 500. Jeff Gordon (No. 24) finishes first, followed by Terry Labonte (No. 5) and Ricky Craven (No. 25).

Earnhardt, angry and determined, had refused medical care and returned to his car to finish the race, finishing in 31st place. The race ended under a yellow caution flag because of a big pileup. Jeff Gordon came in first, the youngest racer to ever win the Daytona 500, Terry Labonte second, and Ricky Craven third. Bobby Labonte came in 21st. Gordon kept his promise to Rick Hendrick to make him smile at the end of the race. Hendrick called his drivers from his cell phone to tell them they'd given him the best medicine he could get.

As of August 1998, Bobby Labonte, for the first time, had moved ahead of Terry in the points standings. He was fifth and Terry was ninth. In 1999 Bobby finished second in points and won a career-best five races, this after breaking his shoulder blade in a crash during a Busch Series practice

Terry Labonte (left), Jeff Gordon (center) and Ricky Craven celebrate their team's 1-2-3 finish at the Daytona 500. They dedicated their extraordinary victory to team owner Rick Hendrick, who was battling leukemia.

session. He stopped racing in the Busch Series after that, but did not miss a Cup start. It was Bobby now dreaming of winning the Cup championship.

In 2000 Bobby's main rivals for the championship were Dale Jarrett and Dale Earnhardt Sr. Bobby took the points lead after the third race of the season at Las Vegas. He dropped down after the April race at Talladega Superspeedway, and went back up again in the following race in California. He won the Brickyard 400 at the Indianapolis Motor Speedway. He was well aware that everyone who had won the Brickyard over the past three years had gone on to become champion.

Bobby knew the championship was his when he finished fourth at Homestead-Miami Speedway when his teammate Tony Stewart won the race. He was thrilled, and began thanking his team members over his radio before the race

Bobby Labonte holds up the trophy he won at the 2003 NASCAR Ford 400 at the Homestead-Miami Speedway in Homestead, Florida. Bobby had won at Homestead in 2000 to capture the Cup championship.

had ended. He and Terry are the first brothers to both win the Cup championship. Bobby is the first driver in history to win a NASCAR Busch Series and NASCAR Cup championship. In 2001 he and Terry had a park named in their honor in Corpus Christi, Texas.

Race Cars Are Not Family Cars

Stock cars have wraparound windshields, a roof, fenders over the wheels, and a trunk in the back—features that make you think of the family car. There are major differences, however. Whereas a Ford or a Chevrolet might cost between $30,000 and $35,000, a NASCAR car costs $120,000. The horsepower/rpm for your car runs around 340 horsepower/5,000 rpm, but a race car's horsepower is 800 and the rpm is 9,000. The top speed for your car is 120 mph, while a race car at Daytona runs at 190 mph. The race car consumes 20 quarts of racing oil at $10 a quart; the average family car takes 5 to 6 quarts of oil every 3,000 to 6,000 miles at $4 a quart. Tires for a race car run $1,500 for a set of four, and 7 to 9 sets are used per car in the Daytona 500. The average lifespan of the tire is 75 to 100 miles. For your car, the tires will last 50,000 miles and will cost around $300 for four.*

Stock car lights are really decals, and the tires lack tread because a smooth surface provides a better grip. Stock cars have no windshield wipers and no doors (drivers crawl in and out of a small window). They have one seat, a steering wheel that detaches so the driver can get in, and a toggle switch on the dash. There is no speedometer, so drivers have to check the rpm instead.

They look like real cars, however, and it is believed that that is one of the many things that attract such huge audiences to the tracks—the illusion that it could be the family car. And that the driver could be you.

*Amy Rosewater, "With Website, Quiet Outsider Emerges as Racing Insider," *USA Today*, February 18, 2005, p. 16F.

Terry, on the other hand, had two crashes in 2000, one in Florida and one in New Hampshire. Diagnosed with a concussion, he did not race in the Brickyard 400 or the Frontier at the Glen. He had never before missed a race. He learned later that he was suffering from an inner ear problem. He finished 17th in the points that year. The next year he finished 23rd, a record he would like to forget. In 2002 he had a career-low finish at 24th in the standings. True to his nature, he continued to race steadily, always trying to improve. And it paid off: in 2003 he ended up 10th in the point standings. He had made his way back into the running.

Bobby won that year at Atlanta Motor Speedway and at Homestead-Miami Speedway, and he ended up in the top 10 as well. He finished eighth in points. In 2001 he finished sixth in points, then went down to 16th in points in 2002.

Sadly, 2004 turned out to be his worst season so far. At the end of the season, Terry announced that he would drive in only 10 races in 2005. He is driving the No. 44 Chevy, and a young driver named Kyle Busch will be stepping into his car after those 10 races. Justin Labonte is driving the No. 44 in the Busch Series.

Bobby also had an awful 2004 season, but it hadn't started out that way. He didn't make the Chase for the Nextel Cup race. He had been 10th in points after 10 races, and there were 11 races to go. The rumor was that something was happening behind the scenes. Bobby's crew chief, Michael "Fatback" McSwain, had left by mid-summer. After that, Bobby began losing steam. He insisted that it had nothing to do with his crew chief leaving.

Both Labonte brothers, along with many whom they had raced with for years, were experiencing more change in their profession than they had in a long time as they entered 2005.

7

AN ERA OF CHANGE

If one word could be applied to NASCAR over the past five years, it would be "change." The name of the Winston Cup has changed to the Nextel Cup. NASCAR wanted to get rid of the old regional image. The sport is the fifth most popular in the world today. The owner of NASCAR, Brian France, is considered one of the 10 richest men in the world. The racing rules have changed. New tracks are being built. The worry is that the new tracks will not have the character of some of the older ones like Darlington Raceway. A wave of drivers is leaving and new ones—labeled the "Top Guns"—are coming in. Another kind of change happened when some of the sport's favorite drivers crashed and died. A new focus on safety appeared in NASCAR. The question remains: how to have men drive cars at death-defying speeds for entertainment and keep them safe?

Though many of the older drivers have been outspoken about their dislike of what is going on overall, the Labonte brothers remain consistent in their goal of remaining in the race world. Bobby is racing full time in 2005. His engine blew in the 2005 Daytona 500, putting him in 44th position. In 2004, Terry announced that he was cutting back. He is only going to run 10 races in 2005, and he can choose which they are. He knows he will not run the Daytona 500. He has

NASCAR tech and safety inspection officials check a race car with a body template before a race. There was a new focus on safety after the death of Dale Earnhardt Sr.

never won it, and he does not want to start the year feeling defeated. He also is not going to run in the race at Talladega Superspeedway. Both the Daytona and the Talladega tracks require using restrictor plates. This causes the cars to bunch up, and then accidents happen.

Terry Labonte isn't alone in his plan to fade out of NASCAR Cup racing. Dale Jarrett, Mark Martin, and Rusty Wallace, all in their mid to late 40s, are pulling out. There is no question that some of them were affected by Dale Earnhardt Sr.'s death during the 2001 Daytona 500. They claim that they want to spend more time with their families.

Bobby Labonte waits by his car before practice at Daytona International Speedway in February 2005. Bobby finished 44th in this Daytona 500 because of a blown engine.

Others are planning to put their energy into their children's racing careers.

Driver Jeff Burton said, " . . . . you start to understand there is a danger in what we do the older we get. That's why I won't do it [overly] long. 'Cause I know that when I'm 43 years old I won't be as effective as I am at 33."[17]

The face of NASCAR is changing. In 2001, Brian France, the grandson of the founder of NASCAR, decided to make a deal worth billions with major television networks. With millions of new fans—and with new sponsors paying as much

Sponsors may pay up to $10 million to sponsor a car. Since 2001, NASCAR guarantees 35 spots to sponsored cars to make sure their advertisements get maximum exposure during television coverage of the races. Corporate logos abound on all things NASCAR.

as $10 million to sponsor a car—NASCAR has to meet their demands. Today, 35 sponsored cars are guaranteed spots in the race to make sure that a sponsor paying millions at least has his advertisement on the track.

France decided to make winning harder. And he upped the cash. Bobby Labonte was the first to win $3,000,000 when he captured the Cup in 2000. Up until 2001, the championship

DID YOU KNOW?

It's About the Money

Hendrick Motorsports has an operating budget of $29 million for three teams. Generally the money comes from sponsors, winnings, auxiliary income, and the owner's personal fortune. Sponsors spend as much as $10 million each year to have their names on the cars.

The drivers are walking advertisements, and their cars are covered with ads. Top drivers spend hundreds of hours each year promoting the sponsors' products, meeting fans, shaking hands, and posing for photographs. There is a bonus in that, too, however: sales for those little car replicas and other toys bring in millions more to the drivers, usually more than they receive from their race wins.

The numbers are posted everywhere. In 2004, Dale Earnhardt Jr. won $7,201,380. Bobby Labonte came in with $4,570,540. Terry Labonte won $3,745,240. As for the newcomers, Kurt Busch won $4,200,330 and Jimmie Johnson brought in $5,692,620. Many of the drivers race in the Busch series, the Truck Craftsman series, and the International Race of Champions for extra cash.

NASCAR itself isn't doing badly. A six-year, $2.8 billion deal was signed with FOX and NBC that put the races onto their stations. Brian France, owner and president of NASCAR, was listed recently as one of the richest men in America.

Gas is free. Unocal provides the racing fuel (108 octane) for free to Cup racers.*

*Jim Wright, *Fixin' to Git: One Man's Love Affair with NASCAR's Winston Cup*, Durham, NC: Duke University Press, p. 131.

NASCAR's "young guns" have been filling the public's demand for new stars. In September 2004, the top 10 drivers in NASCAR Cup points were all under 35 years of age except for Mark Martin. From left in the back are Dale Earnhardt Jr., Matt Kenseth, Tony Stewart, Elliot Sadler, Kurt Busch, and Mark Martin. At bottom from the left are Jeff Gordon, Jimmy Johnson, Jeremy Mayfield, and Ryan Newman.

was won through consistency—the number of points that were accumulated over a season created the winner. That is still in effect for 29 races. However, France added ten races to spark more public interest. No matter how many points a racer has after 29 races, it is one of the top 10 drivers from that group who will win the Nextel Cup. They all start at 0 in the final 10 races. Rusty Wallace and Mark Martin have both said that if NASCAR still had a 29-race schedule instead of 36, they'd be back for another full season.

The young Kurt Busch won the Nextel Cup championship in 2004, the first time the change was in effect. However, if NASCAR had tallied up the points the old way, Jeff Gordon would have had the most.

Columnist Mark McCarter wrote, "Blame NASCAR for turning a once-sensible schedule into an absurd marathon. Blame the gobs of money for forcing drivers and teams into six- and seven-day work weeks and constant travel and testing and the sort of multitasking that turns them into performers juggling chainsaws and bowling balls and lighted tiki torches."[18]

The pressure has always been on the drivers, but the public's demand for stars is never-ending. They want action, and the new "young guns" that are swarming into NASCAR races fill that need. Five drivers in their 20s were first in the 2005 Daytona 500.

Richard Petty said, " . . . . owners get a lot of young drivers coming in who get a lot of pressure on them really, really quick . . . . a lot of these guys figure if they don't prove themselves in the first race or in the first situation they get into, then they're not going to be here very long . . . . it used to be we would recycle drivers."[19]

One of the problems is that many of the racers know they will only get one chance. Drivers like the Labontes spent years building up to their successes. They swept floors, built their own cars, and acted as their own crew chiefs.

Changes are happening on the racetrack, too. As the pressure builds, the younger drivers are a little more reckless. At the 2005 Daytona 500, Jimmie Johnson began blocking Tony Stewart on the banking. Stewart ended up seventh, giving Johnson a pay-back bump on the cool-down lap. NASCAR called them in and they emerged declaring their friendship.[20]

Earlier, in a qualifying race, Johnson became furious when Kevin Harvick bump-drafted him in the middle of a corner. It caused a crash that forced the top contenders out. By the end, Harvick had caused six or seven cars to wreck, knocking some of them out of the competition.

"What happened out there is Kevin Harvick is driving like an idiot," said driver Joe Nemechek.[20] NASCAR made Harvick and Johnson meet to resolve their differences.

Through all the changes that are taking place, Terry and Bobby Labonte remain consistently who they are—"two of the nicest guys you'll ever want to meet," according to NASCAR writer Marty Smith, who has traveled with them. "And two of the funniest," he added.[22]

Terry wants to put his energy into his son Justin now. Steve Solloway brought up the subject of good manners in one of his columns about the group of drivers known more by bad behavior than by good driving. When Justin Labonte won at Chicagoland Speedway, Solloway was impressed: "Instead of spinning his car in celebration or spinning his tires until plumes of smoke filled the sky, Justin Labonte simply pulled up to the start-finish line after his cool-down lap. He waited for the checkered flag. Then, holding it out the window, he lapped the speedway slowly to the crowd's cheers. So understated. So respectful."[23] So like his father and his uncle.

At Terry's semiretirement announcement that he would be leaving NASCAR, Bobby choked back tears as he spoke about his brother. "It's kind of like maybe I should be retiring," Bobby said. Later he added, "I've always wanted to grow up and be like my brother."[24]

The brothers remain best of friends. They park their motor homes next to each other. They eat together, and lean on each other. They go hunting and fishing together.

NASCAR columnist Marty Smith writes, "You'll never hear a fan or industry personality say they don't like Terry or Bobby Labonte."[25]

Rick Hendrick said of the family, "If you want to see a template of professional values and family and what this sport is all about, it's the Labonte family."[26]

Bobby is known for his charity work. He was one of the first drivers to get involved with the Victory Junction Gang Camp, which is a retreat for sick children. It was started by the Petty family after their son Adam was killed. Bobby spoke about giving. "If you put 25 percent away to charities, you get more out of that than you do buying a trick something of the week."[27]

Bobby is just as passionate about his son Tyler's racing career as his brother is about Justin's. He has built a quarter Midget Mecca for him. He is also building a quarter Midget track. Progress is posted on the web. Bobby's daughter Madison wants to race, and the prediction is that the future is opening up for girls and for people of color at NASCAR.

Whatever the Labonte Brothers do, it will be done with style. But it will be their own style. One thing that has not changed at NASCAR is the character and personalities of the Labonte brothers. And that's a good thing.

NOTES

Chapter 1

1. Richard Huff, "Countdown to Championship: Inside NASCAR," September/October 1997, p. 18.

2. Ibid.

Chapter 2

3. *Great Racing Legends: Terry and Bobby Labonte*, Fort Mill, SC: UAV Corporation, 1994.

4. Telephone interview with Slick Yoemans, January 1998.

5. Ibid.

6. *Great Racing Legends: Terry and Bobby Labonte.*

7. Telephone interview with Martha Labonte, January 1998.

Chapter 3

8. Telephone interview with Martha Labonte, January 1998.

Chapter 4

9. Telephone interview with Martha Labonte, January 1998.

10. Telephone interview with Beverly Crotts, January 1998.

11. *Great Racing Legends: Terry and Bobby Labonte.*

Chapter 5

12. Ben White, "Oh Brother!" *Winston Cup Illustrated*, January 1997, p. 102.

13. Bruce Martin, "The History of Bobby Labonte's Drive to the NASCAR Winston Cup Championship: Abnormal consistency and an unshakable demeanor are the secrets to his success," StockCarRacing.com, February 22, 2005, *www.stockcarracing.com/thehistoryof/8214.*

14. Nate Ryan, "Genes and Machines," *Richmond Times Dispatch*, February 13, 2005, p. C1.

Chapter 6

15. Ed Hinton, "True to His Word," *Sports Illustrated Presents the 1997 Winston Cup.* December 3, 1997, p. 25.

16. Marty Smith, "Little brother melts in presence of 'The Iceman,'" NASCAR.com, October 14, 2004, *www.nascar.com/2004/news/opinion/10/14/tlabonte_blabonte/.*

Chapter 7

17. Wayne G. Miller, *Men and Speed: A Wild Ride Through NASCAR's Breakout Season.* New York, NY: Public Affairs, 2002.

18. Mark McCarter, "Backstretch Drivers: Middle-aged generation winding down," February 20, 2005, *www.al.com.*

19. Ibid.

20. Chris Jenkins, "Harvick, Havoc in 500 Qualifying Touch off Criticism," *USA Today*, February 18, 2005, p. C1.

21. Ibid.

22. Marty Smith, "Little brother melts in presence of 'The Iceman.'"

23. Steve Solloway, "Labonte's Been Heard, No Question," MaineToday.com, July 15, 2004, *http://sports.mainetoday.com/pro/autorace/ 040725solloway.shtml.*

24. Marty Smith, "Little brother melts in presence of 'The Iceman.'"

25. Ibid.

26. Ibid.

27. Lee Montgomery, "Conversation: Bobby Labonte," NASCAR.com, June 28, 2004, *www.nascar. com/2004/news/features/conversation/06/28/ blabonte_convo/.*

CHRONOLOGY

Terry Labonte

1956 Born in Corpus Christi, Texas, on November 16.

1963 Starts racing quarter Midgets, later switches to go-karts.

1971 Starts racing late model cars; travels to Houston for races.

1976 Late Model Stock Champ in Houston and San Antonio, Texas; Billy Hagen sponsors him; goes to North Carolina to start racing.

1978 Marries Kim VanMeter; makes racing debut at Southern 500 in Darlington, South Carolina.

1979 Participates in first race of his streak of most consecutive races.

1980 Wins first NASCAR Cup race at Darlington, South Carolina.

1981 Wins first Cup pole position at Hampton, Georgia; son Justin born February 5.

1982 Suffers serious crash in Riverside, California.

1983 Daughter Kristy born June 8.

1984 Wins Cup Championship.

1987 Starts driving for Junior Johnson.

1990   Returns to Billy Hagen's team.

1993   Signs with owner Rick Hendrick at Hendrick Motorsports.

1994   Has first win with Hendrick Motorsports at North Wilkesboro, North Carolina.

1995   Sets record for most consecutive Cup races.

1996   Wins Cup Championship.

1997   Comes in second at Daytona 500; wins Diehard 5090; has seven top-5 finishes.

1998   Comes in second at Food City 500, Bristol Motor Speedway in Bristol, Tennessee.

2000   Crashed in Daytona and New Hampshire; missed the Brickyard 400 and Frontier at Watkins Glen. End of 655 consecutive start streak.

2003   Wins final Southern 500. Came in 10th in points.

2004   Announces semi-retirement for 2005; son Justin Labonte wins first NASCAR Busch Series race.

2005   Will race ten races.

Bobby Labonte

1964 Born in Corpus Christi, Texas, on May 8.

1969 Starts winning races around the country in quarter Midgets.

1979 Starts racing late model stock cars.

1987 Wins Late Model Championship at Caraway Speedway in Caraway, North Carolina.

1988 Wins Late Model Sportsman.

1990 Most Popular Driver in Busch Series.

1991 First NASCAR Cup race at Dover, Delaware; becomes NASCAR Busch Series champion.

1993 Finishes second to Jeff Gordon in Cup Rookie of the Year standings.

1994 In role of car owner (David Green's car), wins Busch Series Championship; son Richard Tyler born April 18.

1995 Wins Coca-Cola 600 at Lowe's Motor Speedway (formerly Charlotte Motor Speedway) in Concord, North Carolina.

1996 Wins NAPA 500 Cup Race in Atlanta, Georgia.

1997 Wins NAPA 500 Cup Race; has eight top finishes.

1998 Wins Primestar 500 at Atlanta Motor Speedway; wins Diehard 500 in Talladega, Alabama; daughter Madison Elizabeth born January 15.

2000 Wins Cup championship (in first 24 races, had 17 top-10 and 13 top-5 finishes); selected Driver of the Year for all American Motorsports. Also carries the fan vote.

2003 Finishes ninth in the points.

2004 Finishes 12th in the points.

2005 Racing full time.

STATISTICS

Terry Labonte's Cup Statistics:

Year	Wins	Top 5	Top 10	Pole	Earnings
1978	0	1	3	0	$ 21,395
1979	0	2	13	0	134,652
1980	1	6	16	0	222,501
1981	0	8	17	2	348,703
1982	0	17	21	2	398,635
1983	1	11	20	3	388,419
1984	2	17	24	2	767,716
1985	1	8	17	4	694,509
1986	1	5	10	1	522,235
1987	1	13	22	4	805,054
1988	1	11	18	1	950,781
1989	2	9	11	0	703,806
1990	0	4	9	0	450,230
1991	0	1	7	1	348,898
1992	0	4	16	0	600,381
1993	0	0	10	0	531,717
1994	3	6	14	0	1,125,921
1995	3	14	17	1	1,558,659
1996	2	21	24	4	4,030,648
1997	1	8	20	0	2,270,144
1998	1	5	15	0	2,054,163
1999	1	1	7	0	2,475,365
2000	0	3	6	1	2,239,716
2001	0	1	3	0	3,011,901
2002	0	1	4	0	3,244,240
2003	1	4	9	1	3,643,690
2004	0	0	6	0	3,745,242
2005	0	0	0	0	76,550
Total	**22**	**181**	**359**	**27**	**$37,365,871**

Statistics taken from *www.racing-reference.com*.

Bobby Labonte's Cup Statistics:

Year	Wins	Top 5	Top 10	Pole	Earnings
1991	0	0	0	0	$ 8,530
1993	0	0	6	1	395,660
1994	0	1	2	0	550,305
1995	3	7	14	2	1,413,682
1996	1	5	14	4	1,475,196
1997	1	9	18	3	2,217,999
1998	2	11	18	3	2,980,052
1999	5	23	26	5	4,763,615
2000	4	19	24	2	7,361,386
2001	2	9	20	1	4,786,779
2002	1	5	7	0	4,183,715
2003	2	12	17	4	4,745,260
2004	0	5	11	1	5,201,397
2005	0	0	0	0	382,081
Total	**404**	**21**	**106**	**26**	**$40,465,477**

Statistics taken from *www.racing-reference.com.*

FURTHER READING

Bernstein, Viv. "The New Face of NASCAR: Ruling Family's Next Generation Changes the Sport." *The New York Times*, February 20, 2005.

Bigelow, Big. "Terry Labonte to Run Part-Time for the Next Two Seasons; Tiger Sportsman Gets His Say." CaledonianRecord.com, October 14, 2004. *www. caledonianrecord.com/pages/strap_in/story/ad86a1355.*

Burt, Bill. *Behind the Scenes of NASCAR Racing.* Osceola, WI: MBI Publishing Corporation, 1997.

Gabbard, Alex. *Indy's Wildest Decade: Innovation and Revolution at the Brickyard.* North Branch, MN: CarTech, 2004.

Golenbock, Peter. *The Last Lap.* New York, NY: Hungry Minds, Incorporated, 2001.

———. *NASCAR Confidential: Stories of the Men and Women who Made Stock Car Racing Great.* St. Paul, MN: MBI Publishing Corporation, 2004.

Griffith, Bill. "Fox is all Aglow over Daytona." *Boston Sunday Globe*, February 20, 2005.

Harris, Mike. "Rookie Speeds to Pole." *The News & Observer*, February 27, 2005.

Hinton, Ed. *Daytona: From the Birth of Speed to the Death of the Man in Black.* New York, NY: Warner Books, 2001.

Long, Mark. "NASCAR Keeps Searching for Young Talent." *The Associated Press*, February 26, 2005. *http://news.enquirer.com/apps/pbcs.dll/article?AID=/20050226/SPT/502260381/1062.*

Martin, Mark, and Beth Tuschak. *NASCAR for Dummies*. Hoboken, NJ: John Wiley & Sons, 2005.

Menzer, Joe. *The Wildest Ride: A History of NASCAR*. New York, NY: Simon & Schuster, 2001.

Montgomery, Lee. "Changing of the Guard: As older drivers depart, young stars are filling the void." *The News & Observer*, February 12, 2005.

———. "In Review: B. Labonte." NASCAR.com, December 12, 2004. *www.nascar.com/2004/news/headlines/cup/12/12/blabonte_inreview/index.html.*

———. "Labonte, Bowyer reach Texas in different ways." NASCAR.com, April 1, 2004. *www.nascar.com/2004/news/headlines/bg/04/01/preview_texas/index.html.*

Montville, Leigh. *At the Altar of Speed: The Fast Life and Tragic Death of Dale Earnhardt*. New York, NY: Doubleday, 2001.

Sowers, Richard. *Stock Car Racing Lives*. Phoenix, AZ: David Bull, 2000.

Sporting News editors. *NASCAR Record and Fact Book: 2005 Edition*. New York, NY: Sporting News Books, 2005.

Tyler, Lori. "Justin Labonte Nets First Busch Win." CatchFence.com, July 12, 2004. *http://catchfence.com/html/2004/lt071204.html.*

Vega, Michael. "Lepage comes up big for little guys." *The Boston Globe*, February 19, 2005.

Waltrip, Darrell, and Jade Gurss. *DW: A Lifetime of Going Around in Circles*. New York, NY: G.F. Putnam's Sons, 2004.

Yates, Brock. *NASCAR Off the Record*. St. Paul, MN: MBI Publishing Corporation, 2004.

BIBLIOGRAPHY

Assael, Shaun. *Wide Open: Days and Nights on the NASCAR Tour.* New York, NY: Ballantine Books, 1998.

Great Racing Legends: Terry and Bobby Labonte, Fort Mill, SC: UAV Corporation, 1994.

Hinton, Ed. "True to His Word," *Sports Illustrated Presents the 1997 Winston Cup.* December 3, 1997.

Huff, Richard. "Countdown to Championship: Inside NASCAR," September/October 1997.

Jenkins, Chris. "Harvick, Havoc in 500 Qualifying Touch off Criticism," *USA Today*, February 18, 2005.

Jenson, Tom. *Cheating: An Inside Look at the Bad Things Good NASCAR Nextel Cup Racers Do in Pursuit of Speed.* Pheonix, AZ: David Bull Publishing, 2004.

Martin, Bruce. "The History of Bobby Labonte's Drive to the NASCAR Winston Cup Championship: Abnormal consistency and an unshakable demeanor are the secrets to his success," StockCarRacing.com, February 22, 2005, *www.stockcarracing.com/ thehistoryof/8214.*

McCarter, Mark. "Backstretch Drivers: Middle-aged generation winding down," February 20, 2005, *www.al.com.*

Miller, Wayne G. *Men and Speed: A Wild Ride Through NASCAR's Breakout Season.* New York, NY: Public Affairs, 2002.

Montgomery, Lee. "Conversation: Bobby Labonte," NASCAR.com, June 28, 2004, *www.nascar.com/2004/ news/features/conversation/06/28/blabonte_convo/.*

"NASCAR: Drivers take stock of their fitness," *Knight Ridder Tribune*, February 9, 2005, *www.freep.com/ sports/othersports/autos9e_20050209.htm.*

Rosewater, Amy. "With Website, Quiet Outsider Emerges as Racing Insider." *USA Today*, February 18, 2005.

Ryan, Nate. "Genes and Machines," *Richmond Times Dispatch*, February 13, 2005.

Smith, Marty. "Little brother melts in presence of 'The Iceman,'" NASCAR.com, October 14, 2004, *www.nascar. com/2004/news/opinion/10/14/tlabonte_blabonte/.*

Solloway, Steve. "Labonte's Been Heard, No Question," MaineToday.com, July 15, 2004, *http://sports. mainetoday.com/pro/autorace/040725solloway.shtml.*

White, Ben. "Oh Brother!" *Winston Cup Illustrated*, January 1997.

Wright, Jim. *Fixin' to Git: One fan's love affair with NASCAR's Winston Cup*. Durham, NC: Duke University Press, 2002.

ADDRESSES

Atlanta Motor Speedway
P.O. Box 500
Hampton, GA 30228
(770) 946-4211

Daytona International Speedway
P.O. Box 2801
Daytona Beach, FL 32120-2801
(386) 254-2700

Joe Gibbs Racing
13415 Reese Blvd. West
Huntersville, NC 28078

National Association for Stock Car Auto Racing
    (NASCAR)
P.O. Box 2875
Daytona Beach, FL 32120
(386) 253-0611

Photo Credits:

INTERNET SITES

www.bobbylabonte.com

> *This is the official website for racer Bobby Labonte.*

www.joegibbsracing.com

> *This website is dedicated to Joe Gibbs Racing.*

www.labonteonline.com

> *This is website is home to Bobby, Justin, and Terry Labonte.*

www.nascar.com

> *This website is the best place to start learning more about NASCAR (National Association for Stock Car Auto Racing). It has the latest results and driver standings, but there are also pages where readers can learn more about the sport in general.*

www.hendrickmotorsports.com

> *This is the official site of Hendrick Motorsports NASCAR Racing & Team Store.*

www.stockcarracing.com

> *This is the* Stock Car Racing *magazine website.*

www.terrylabonte.net

> *This is the official website for racer Terry Labonte.*

INDEX

ABOUT THE AUTHOR

Janet Hubbard-Brown has written many books, both fiction and non-fiction, for children and young adults. She grew up in a family in South Hill, Virginia, where Rick Hendrick was a regular guest.